NATURE'S ULTIMATE DISASTERS

TOP 10 WORST
HURRICANES

Louise and Richard Spilsbury

PowerKiDS
press

New York

Published in 2017 by
The Rosen Publishing Group, Inc.
29 East 21st Street, New York, NY 10010

Cataloging-in-Publication Data

Names: Spilsbury, Louise.
Title: Top 10 worst hurricanes / Louise and Richard Spilsbury.
Description: New York : PowerKids Press, 2017. | Series: Nature's ultimate disasters | Includes index.
Identifiers: ISBN 9781499430776 (pbk.) | ISBN 9781499430790 (library bound) | ISBN 9781499430783 (6 pack)
Subjects: LCSH: Hurricanes--Juvenile literature. | Hurricane damage--Juvenile literature.
Classification: LCC QC944.2 S65 2017 | DDC 363.34'922--dc23

Produced for Rosen by Calcium
Editors for Calcium Creative Ltd: Sarah Eason and Harriet McGregor
Designers: Paul Myerscough and Simon Borrough
Picture research: Rachel Blount

Picture credits: Cover: Shutterstock: Glynnis Jones; Inside: NOAA: Debbie Larson, NWS, International Activities 17;
Shutterstock: Michael Ciranni 1, KAZMAT 23, Leonard Zhukovsky 4–5, Zstock 6–7; Wikimedia Commons: U.S. Coast Guard
photo by Petty Officer 2nd Class NyxoLyno Cangemi 13, Sonny Day 15, NASA/Joint Typhoon Warning Center 11, NOAA 19,
21, Presidencia de la República Mexicana 25, Eoghan Rice/Trócaire/Caritas 27, Image courtesy of Mike Trenchard, Earth
Sciences & Image Analysis Laboratory, Johnson Space Center 7, Library of Congress/Zahner, MH 9.

Manufactured in the United States of America

CPSIA Compliance Information: Batch #BW17PK: For Further Information contact Rosen Publishing, New York, New York at 1-800-237-9932.

Contents

Hurricane Danger 4

Hurricanes in Action 6

10 Great Galveston Hurricane ..8

9 Typhoon Nina 10

8 Hurricane Katrina 12

7 Typhoon Bopha 14

6 Hurricane Mitch 16

5 Typhoon Tip 18

4 Hurricane Camille 20

3 Labor Day Hurricane 22

2 Hurricane Patricia...............24

1 Typhoon Haiyan..................26

Where in the World? 28

Glossary 30

Further Reading 31

Index....................................32

HURRICANE DANGER

Hurricanes are the deadliest and most powerful storms on Earth. They form over warm ocean waters, but can blow toward land. They bring fast winds and heavy rains that cause terrible destruction.

How Dangerous?

It is hard to tell exactly how fast the winds in a hurricane blow, because these deadly storms often damage measuring equipment. Hurricane winds range from speeds of 75 miles (120 km) per hour to more than 150 miles (240 km) per hour. The worst, most dangerous hurricane winds may reach 200 miles (320 km) per hour. Hurricane winds can flatten buildings, snap power lines, pull up trees, and bring rain that causes devastating **floods**. In the ocean, the winds cause huge waves that throw boats and ships around like toys. They may even toss ships up onto the shore.

More than 80 houses were destroyed in Breezy Point, New York, by a fire that broke out when Hurricane Sandy swept through the area.

Measuring Disaster

Scientists use a number of techniques to detect hurricanes and figure out where they might hit the coast, so they can warn people to **evacuate**.

Scientists must get inside hurricanes to understand how they work.

→

Drones are flying machines. They fly into the **eye** of a hurricane and collect information about how hurricanes develop.

Hurricanes begin as thunderclouds.

→

Scientists use pictures of clouds taken by weather **satellites** high above Earth's surface to figure out which clouds might become hurricanes.

Hurricanes can travel long distances.

→

Meteorologists use powerful computers called supercomputers to analyze billions of pieces of weather information from around the world. This helps them predict where hurricanes might happen.

Natural disasters have taken place since Earth was formed. People have many ways of deciding what the world's worst natural disasters have been, from the deadliest disaster to the costliest. This book includes some of the worst disasters in history.

The Saffir-Simpson Hurricane Scale ranks hurricanes from 1 to 5 based on wind speed and the damage they could cause. The least dangerous is 1 and the most dangerous is 5. This gives people a quick and clear idea of what is coming when warnings are given. Hurricanes are also named to identify them. Hurricanes are named in alphabetical order but the names never begin with the letters Q, U, X, Y, or Z because few names start with these letters.

Palm trees such as these are able to bend in high winds, but hurricane force winds can completely destroy them.

Hurricane, Typhoon, or Cyclone?

Hurricanes form over tropical oceans where the surface water is warm. In some places, hurricanes are known by different names. "Hurricane" is used in the Atlantic and Northeast Pacific Oceans. In the Northwest Pacific a hurricane is called a typhoon, and in the South Pacific and Indian Ocean a hurricane is called a cyclone.

How Hurricanes Form

1. Hurricanes start to form when storm clouds move over warm ocean water.

2. The warm ocean water warms the air above it. As the air warms, it starts to rise.

3. Water at the surface of the ocean **evaporates** into **water vapor**. This also rises into the air.

4. As these areas of moving air and clouds rise, they move faster and faster. They start to rotate in a spiral.

This is an image of a hurricane showing its swirling clouds and eye at the center. The picture was taken from a satellite high above planet Earth.

5. The center of the hurricane is calm. It is called the hurricane eye.

6. When hurricanes move away from warm areas of water and toward cooler areas of land, the water vapor they carry **condenses** and turns to liquid. This water falls as rain.

10 GREAT GALVESTON HURRICANE

The Great Galveston Hurricane of 1900 was one of the deadliest natural disasters that has ever happened in the history of the United States. Estimates of the number of people killed range from 6,000 to 12,000.

Galveston

Galveston, Texas

The deadly weather system that caused this hurricane was first spotted on August 27, over the Atlantic Ocean. It reached Cuba as a **tropical storm** on September 3, and moved into the southeastern Gulf of Mexico on September 5. As it headed west-northwest, it grew stronger and stronger. When it hit the island city of Galveston on the Texas coast late on September 8, it was a category 4 hurricane, the second-strongest on the Saffir-Simpson Hurricane Scale.

On the Record

The hurricane caused **storm tides** 8–15 feet (2.5–4.5 m) high. The water flooded into the low-lying city of Galveston and other areas of the nearby Texas coast.

The hurricane winds blew at over 130 miles (210 km) per hour. Homes and businesses were devastated by the floods and wind. The damage to property was estimated at $30 million.

People along the Gulf Coast were warned that a hurricane was coming, but many ignored the warnings.

After making **landfall** at Galveston, the storm moved on through the Great Plains to the Great Lakes and New England, which experienced strong wind gusts and heavy rainfall.

Before the hurricane, Galveston was an important seaport. After the hurricane, Galveston built a large wall to protect against future storms, but it was too late. By then, Houston had become the most important port in Texas.

9 TYPHOON NINA

In August 1975, a typhoon struck China that was intense and devastating. In the short time that Typhoon Nina made landfall, it caused dams to collapse. This led to terrible floods downstream, killing more than 26,000 people immediately and causing the deaths of thousands more people in the following days and weeks.

Typhoon Nina

Heavy Rains

The weather system that caused Typhoon Nina began in the Philippine Sea on July 29. It passed through Taiwan, where it killed 25 people, and hit China on August 3. By August 5, it reached the Henan region, where it stayed for three days. The storm dropped more rain on Henan in that time than usually falls on the region in a whole year.

On the Record

Satellite images like this one show Typhoon Nina's progress as it passed over China.

CHINA

The rainwater from Typhoon Nina fell at a record rate of 7.5 inches (19 cm) per hour.

The huge Banqiao Dam on the Ru River was 387 feet (118 m) tall and held back about 17.4 billion cubic feet (492 million cu m) of water. It collapsed because it could not release water as fast as its **reservoir** was filling.

The typhoon's heavy rains made more than 60 dams and reservoirs collapse, causing many more terrible floods.

When Banqiao Dam collapsed, a wall of water 33 feet (10 m) high and 7 miles (11 km) wide rushed down the river channel at 30 miles (50 km) per hour. The 10,000 inhabitants of the town of Daowencheng were killed instantly.

As well as those killed in floods, 145,000 people died from diseases caught by using river water **contaminated** by the floods or from starvation after crops were ruined.

8 HURRICANE KATRINA

Hurricane Katrina formed during the United States' 2005 Atlantic hurricane season. It was a category 5 hurricane and killed 1,850 people. At the time, it was the deadliest hurricane to have hit the United States for 75 years.

Hurricane Katrina

Gaining Strength

Hurricane Katrina formed over the Caribbean Sea on August 23, and made landfall in Florida on August 25, where it killed nine people. Next, it moved to the Gulf of Mexico, where the warm waters helped it double in size. By the time it reached New Orleans early in the morning of August 29, its wind speeds were 125 miles (200 km) per hour and it was dropping torrential rain.

On the Record

The winds from Hurricane Katrina snapped trees, blasted out windows, and tossed furniture from homes onto the streets. Broken power lines caused fires.

New Orleans lies below **sea level** and had banks of earth called levees built around it to prevent flooding. However, the heavy rains caused such severe flooding that the levees broke and water flooded 80 percent of the city.

In some places in New Orleans, flood waters were 20 feet (6 m) deep.

Seawater filled homes and the water carried venomous snakes, dirt, rocks, and **debris** from damaged buildings all over the city.

As Hurricane Katrina moved along the coast, it caused more damage in Louisiana, Mississippi, and Alabama. It tossed boats ashore and filled towns with mud and sand. In the coastal town of Biloxi, a **storm surge** 30 feet (9 m) high killed 30 people.

13

7 TYPHOON BOPHA

On December 3, 2012, Typhoon Bopha blasted the island of Mindanao in the Philippines. It was the most expensive storm to make landfall in the Philippines and cost the country $1 billion.

Typhoon Bopha

A Vulnerable Country

The Philippines gets a lot of typhoons because it is located in the middle of a huge area of warm water in the Pacific Ocean. The country consists of more than 7,000 islands, which are vulnerable to flooding when typhoons cause storm surges. The large southern island of Mindanao is rarely in the direct path of typhoons. In 2012, its luck ran out.

Typhoon Bopha rated category 5 on the Saffir-Simpson Hurricane Scale and was so powerful that it was called a super typhoon. Millions of people were in the storm's path.

The high winds, flooding, and **landslides** caused by heavy rains from Typhoon Bopha killed around 1,900 people and affected over 6.2 million more.

Trees were uprooted and fragile houses were blown away on Mindanao.

Over 9.4 inches (24 cm) of rain fell near the coast of eastern Mindanao, where the typhoon first hit the island.

The typhoon brought wind gusts of 130 miles (210 km) per hour. People said wind blew corrugated iron roofs from buildings and threw them through the air like "flying machetes."

In the hardest-hit areas, almost 95 percent of the roads, homes, and crops were destroyed.

6 HURRICANE MITCH

Hurricane Mitch devastated parts of Central America in late October, 1998. It rated 5 on the Saffir-Simpson Hurricane Scale for more than 33 hours, making it one of the most dangerous and destructive hurricanes ever recorded.

Hurricane Mitch

Deadly Rains

The storm killed more than 11,000 people, mainly in Honduras and Nicaragua, but also in Guatemala, El Salvador, Mexico, and Costa Rica. Thousands more were left missing, presumed dead. Most of the people who died were killed in the terrible floods caused by the enormous amount of rain that the storm released. The heavy rains caused more than 50 rivers to flood.

On the Record

Hurricane Mitch moved slowly over land from October 29 to November 3, and released up to 4 inches (10 cm) of rain per hour. In some places, almost 6 feet (2 m) of rain fell during that time.

The heavy rains washed earth into rivers, blocking them and causing floods that washed away people, buildings, roads, and bridges.

This flood damage along the Choluteca River was caused by Hurricane Mitch.

The floods and landslides damaged many thousands of other homes and buildings, leaving millions of people without somewhere to live.

The heavy rains caused a lake filling the crater at the top of Casita volcano, in Nicaragua, to overflow. This made the sides of the volcano collapse. The landslide completely buried at least four villages around the volcano and killed up to 2,000 people.

5 TYPHOON TIP

On October 12, 1979, Typhoon Tip became a record-breaking typhoon. It was a category 5 super typhoon and it was enormous. It had a diameter of 1,350 miles (2,173 km), which is almost half the area of the mainland United States. At its peak, while the typhoon swirled over the open waters of the western Pacific, the eye of Typhoon Tip was over 9 miles (15 km) wide.

Typhoon Tip

Fast and Furious

Tip was the strongest typhoon to hit Japan's main island in over 10 years. At their fastest, winds from Tip blew at 190 miles (306 km) per hour. Luckily, the typhoon's strength and speed dropped before it hit the heavily populated regions of southern Japan, avoiding a high death toll. Typhoon Tip killed 86 people but injured hundreds more.

Tip caused widespread flooding that destroyed more than 20,000 homes in Japan. Over 11,000 people were left homeless. The heavy rains also caused 600 landslides in the mountains.

A total of 40 US Air Force missions flew into Typhoon Tip, making it one of the most closely studied typhoons in history.

Typhoon Tip made tall buildings in the capital city, Tokyo, sway from side to side.

Typhoon Tip's winds blew over a gasoline storage tank, causing an explosion and fire that spread quickly through a US Marine Corps camp at Mount Fuji. The fire killed 13 people and injured dozens more.

HURRICANE CAMILLE

4

Hurricane Camille formed from a tropical storm that started in the Caribbean, west of the Cayman Islands, on August 14, 1969. By the time it hit Bay Saint Louis in Mississippi shortly before midnight on August 17, it was a powerful category 5 hurricane.

Hurricane Camille

Storm Warnings

Although meteorologists could not be sure what path the hurricane would take, they warned more than 150,000 people to evacuate their homes. Most people followed the advice and left the danger zones in time. Some people stayed and more than 250 of them were killed.

On the Record

Camille's gales were so strong they knocked out all wind-recording equipment. Experts estimate that its wind speeds peaked at more than 200 miles (320 km) per hour. The high winds reduced many buildings to rubble.

Hurricane Camille created waves in the Gulf of Mexico that were more than 70 feet (21 m) high.

Hurricane Camille was one of the strongest hurricanes to hit the United States and it wrecked even huge ships like these.

Before the hurricane moved out into the Atlantic Ocean on August 20, Camille dropped 12–20 inches (30–50 cm) of rain in parts of Virginia. It created floods and mudslides along the foothills of the Blue Ridge Mountains.

After Hurricane Camille, people from the Gulf Coast complained that warnings did not give clear information about how strong hurricanes were expected to be, so the Saffir-Simpson Hurricane Scale was created.

3 LABOR DAY HURRICANE

The Labor Day Hurricane on September 2, 1935, was the third most powerful hurricane in US history. The hurricane's destruction was mainly focused on the Florida Keys area, where it caused a path of devastation 40 miles (64 km) wide.

Labor Day Hurricane

Too Late to Escape

The hurricane began as a weak tropical storm east of the Bahamas. It grew bigger and stronger as it headed west over the warm waters of the Gulf Stream. Forecasters thought it was heading south, and by the time they realized otherwise, it was too late to evacuate people. When the hurricane made landfall at the Florida Keys, a chain of small islands off the southern coast of Florida, it was a deadly and destructive category 5 hurricane.

On the Record

Experts estimate that winds of up to 200 miles (320 km) per hour blew near and over the Florida Keys, with some gusts even faster than that.

The hurricane caused a strong storm tide consisting of a wall of water about 18 feet (5.5 m) high.

The storm tide washed up onto the Keys and destroyed buildings, roads, viaducts, and bridges.

The hurricane killed at least 485 people. About half were residents and visitors. The other half were World War I (1914–1918) **veterans** who were living in tent camps, helping to build bridges between the islands.

The high winds and storm tide also destroyed railroad tracks and even swept a train off its tracks. The 11-car train had been sent to evacuate about 260 of the World War I veterans working in the area. All but the locomotive engine were washed off the tracks.

2 HURRICANE PATRICIA

In 2015, the category 5 Hurricane Patricia became the strongest hurricane to reach Mexico in more than 50 years. It blasted the coast with winds of over 200 miles (320 km) per hour and was one of the most powerful hurricanes ever recorded.

Hurricane Patricia

Powerful Patricia

In 2015, the eastern Pacific was warmer than usual, which may have contributed to the power of Hurricane Patricia. Fortunately, the hurricane did not hit large population centers and people were warned in time to evacuate. This meant that, although Hurricane Patricia was ferocious, it killed only six people.

On the Record

Mexican authorities warned all towns and villages in Patricia's path to evacuate. Thousands of tourists and local people left the danger zone and moved into shelters.

Airports were closed and homes and storefronts were barricaded for protection.

Overall, more than 10,000 homes were damaged or destroyed by Hurricane Patricia.

Around 156 square miles (405 sq km) of farmland were affected and plantain, banana, and papaya crops were ruined.

Strong winds tore roofs off houses; pulled up, snapped, and stripped nearly all trees; and left hillsides bare. Power poles and transmission towers were crumpled by the winds.

Heavy rains caused widespread flooding and even more houses were flooded as rivers burst their banks.

TYPHOON HAIYAN

1

An average of 20 typhoons hit the Philippines each year but Haiyan was more memorable than most. Typhoon Haiyan is one of the most powerful tropical cyclones ever recorded, if not the most powerful, to strike land.

Typhoon Haiyan

A Force of Nature

When Haiyan, known locally as Yulonda, made landfall on November 8, 2013, it was a category 5 hurricane. Its wind blasted the area at speeds of around 195 miles (315 km) per hour. The winds, floods, and storm surge caused by Haiyan killed 7,300 people and destroyed many of the country's coastal farming and fishing communities.

On the Record

Typhoon Haiyan caused a storm surge that was so huge and powerful that it washed ships onto the shore and rolled a rock bigger than a blue whale up a beach.

The storm surge forced a wall of water 25 feet (7.5 m) high into the city of Tacloban, on the northeast tip of the island of Leyte. The island is only 16 feet (5 m) above sea level. The water washed away people and buildings, leaving muddy ground and debris in its wake.

Haiyan, and two tropical storms that passed through the area around the same time, released huge amounts of rain on the central Philippines. Some parts of Leyte got as much as 27 inches (70 cm) of rain.

The central Philippines were worst hit, but more than 16 million people in total were affected by the event in Palau, the Philippines, Vietnam, and China.

More people died in the city of Tacloban than in any other part of the Philippines.

27

WHERE IN THE WORLD?

This map shows the location of the hurricanes, typhoons, and cyclones featured in this book.

ATLANTIC OCEAN

Hurricane Katrina

Hurricane Camille

Great Galveston Hurricane

Labor Day Hurricane

Hurricane Patricia

Hurricane Mitch

PACIFIC OCEAN

Read the case studies about Haiyan (2013), the number 1 typhoon in this book, and Great Galveston (1900), which is number 10. How do they differ?

What facts can you find in this book to support the argument that human actions can affect the amount of damage inflicted by hurricanes?

Why do meteorologists classify storms? What evidence is there in this book that classifying hurricanes can help people?

Typhoon Tip

Typhoon Nina

Typhoon Bopha

Typhoon Haiyan

INDIAN
OCEAN

Where and how do hurricanes form? What makes them stronger and bigger?

How would you explain the difference between a hurricane, a cyclone, and a typhoon?

GLOSSARY

condenses Turns from a gas to a liquid.

contaminated Made dirty or poisonous.

dams Barriers built to hold back river waters and raise their levels.

debris Loose, waste material.

drones Flying machines that are controlled remotely and can do tasks such as take photographs from the air.

evacuate To get away from an area that is dangerous to somewhere that is safe.

evaporates Turns from a liquid into a gas.

eye The calm center of a hurricane.

floods When areas of land that are usually dry are suddenly covered in water.

hurricane season The time of year when hurricanes usually happen.

landfall Reaching land.

landslides Collapses of masses of earth or rock from mountains or cliffs.

meteorologists Scientists who study the weather.

reservoir An artificial lake where water is collected and stored, often behind a dam.

Saffir-Simpson Hurricane Scale The scale by which the strength of a hurricane, typhoon, or cyclone is measured.

satellites Objects in space that travel around Earth.

sea level The average height of the ocean's surface.

storm surge An abnormal rise of water generated by a hurricane or other storm.

storm tides The rise in water level due to the combination of storm surges and the tides.

tropical storm A powerful storm that begins in the tropics. Its winds are not as strong as those of a hurricane.

veterans People who fought in a war.

water vapor Water in the form of gas.

FURTHER READING

Books

Baker, John R. *The World's Worst Hurricanes* (World's Worst Natural Disasters). North Mankato, MN: Capstone, 2016.

Burgan, Michael. *Total Devastation: The Story of Hurricane Katrina* (Tangled History). North Mankato, MN: Capstone, 2016.

Pratt, Mary. *Hurricane Katrina and the Flooding of New Orleans* (Cause-And-Effect Disasters). Minneapolis, MN: Lerner Publications, 2016.

Winchester, Simon. *When the Sky Breaks: Hurricanes, Tornadoes, and the Worst Weather in the World*. New York, NY: Viking Books for Young Readers, 2017.

Websites

Due to the changing nature of Internet links, PowerKids Press has developed an online list of websites related to the subject of this book. This site is updated regularly. Please use this link to access the list: **www.powerkidslinks.com/nud/hurricanes**

INDEX

B

buildings, 4, 13, 15, 17, 19, 21, 27

C

clouds, 5, 7
crops, 11, 15, 25
cyclone, 6, 26, 28–29

D

dams, 10–11
drones, 5

E

evacuate, 5, 20, 22–25

F

fires, 13, 19
floods, 4, 9, 11, 13–17, 19, 21, 25–26

G

Great Galveston Hurricane, 8–9, 28–29
gusts, 9, 15, 23

H

homes, 9, 13, 15, 17, 19–20, 25
Hurricane Camille, 20–21, 29
Hurricane Katrina, 12–13, 29
Hurricane Mitch, 16–17, 29
Hurricane Patricia, 24–25, 29

L

Labor Day Hurricane, 22–23, 29
landslides, 15, 17, 19
levees, 13

M

meteorologists, 5, 20, 29

O

ocean, 4, 6–8, 14, 21

P

port, 9
power lines, 4, 13

R

rains, 4, 7, 9–13, 15–17, 19, 21, 25, 27

S

Saffir-Simpson Hurricane Scale, 6, 8, 15, 16, 21
satellites, 5
starvation, 11
storm surge, 13–14, 26–27
storm tides, 9, 23

T

thunderclouds, 5
tide, 9, 23
trees, 4, 13, 25
typhoon, 6, 10–11, 14–15, 18–19, 26–29
Typhoon Bopha, 14–15, 28
Typhoon Haiyan, 26–28
Typhoon Nina, 10–11, 28
Typhoon Tip, 18–19, 29

W

warnings, 6, 20–21, 24–25
waves, 4, 21
winds, 4, 6, 9, 12–13, 15, 18–19, 21, 23–26

LITTLE RED RIDING HOOD
REIMAGINED!

BY
Jerry Popowich
& Doug Sinclair

ILLUSTRATED BY
Maria Kiriakova

ISBN 978-0-99376-692-3

INSTRUCTIONS

1

DOWNLOAD THE FREE MOBILE APP!

Scan the QR code or visit www.incredebooks.com/apps. Look for the Little Red Riding Hood - Reimagined app and download the app on your iOS or Android device.

2

READ, THEN LOOK FOR SPECIAL PAGES!

Read the book and look for this symbol on special pages. There are four pages that contain special 3D games!

3

WATCH THE PAGES COME TO LIFE IN 3D!

Launch the app and hold your smart phone or tablet facing the book page that contains the symbol. Make sure the entire page is visible. Now watch the page come to life in 3D!

FIND OUT MORE INFORMATION AT WWW.INCREDEBOOKS.COM

There once was a girl named Little Red Riding Hood.
Every day, she'd go skipping through the woods
to visit her grandma.
Really, though, this story isn't about her.
She's not even mentioned on the next few pages at all.

2

This story is really about who she met along the way.
His name was Big Bad Wolf.
But two of the three words in his name
were completely wrong.

The Wolf wasn't very big as far as wolves go,
and he certainly wasn't bad.
He was actually quite nice if anyone bothered
to get to know him.
So, why his mother named him Big Bad,
we will never know.

4

The Wolf was very lonely.
There were no other wolves in the forest,
and all the bunnies and squirrels thought
Big Bad only wanted to be friends with
them because they were
bite-sized and tasted nice with potatoes.

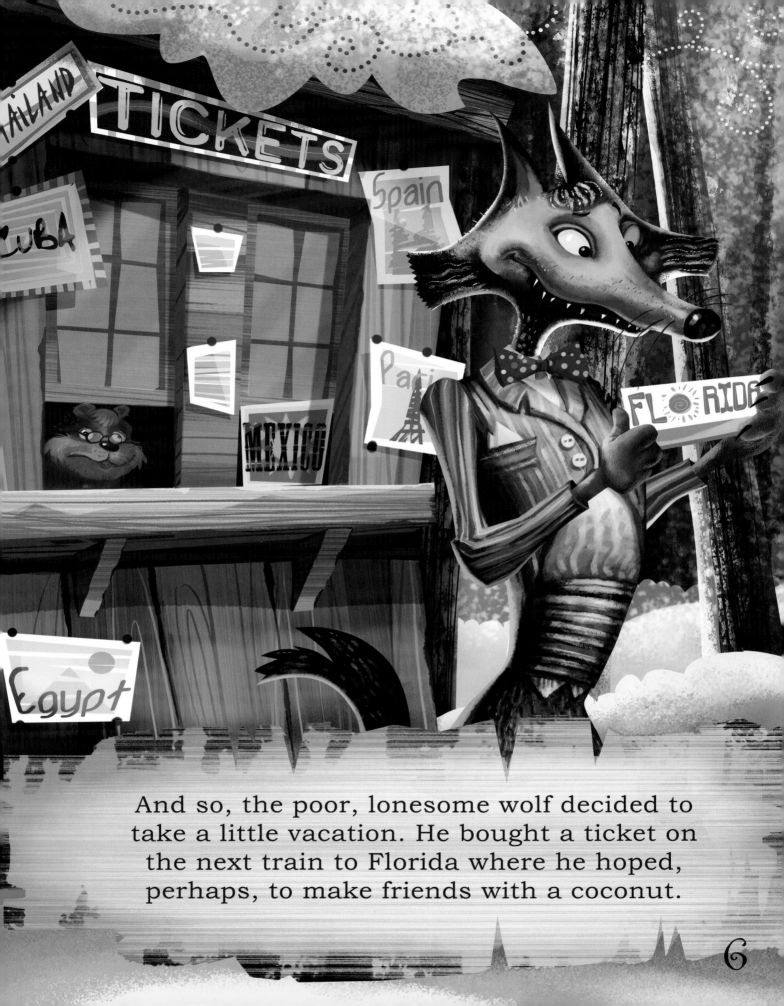

And so, the poor, lonesome wolf decided to take a little vacation. He bought a ticket on the next train to Florida where he hoped, perhaps, to make friends with a coconut.

On his way to the train station, he met
Little Red Riding Hood. She was very friendly,
and her hood blocked most of her eyesight.
So, instead of running away from him screaming,
as most people did, she stopped to chat.

"I'm going to my Grandma's house!" she said.
"It's the very first house in the next village,
and she never locks her door!"
(This is far more information than it's usually
smart to give to a predatory animal).

8

The wolf was amazed.
A nice little girl had spoken to him kindly,
in words that sounded nothing like screams
of terror. This had never, ever happened before,
and he liked it. He liked it a lot!

He wanted to talk to her again!
More than anything else in the world,
Big Bad, that poor sad wolf, wanted a friend.

So, he ran off through the woods following
a shortcut that would get him
to Grandma's house first.

When he got to Grandma's house, she looked unhappy, and she didn't have her glasses on. So, instead of a wolf, she thought he was just a nice stranger who had let himself in and smelled oddly wolf-like. "What's wrong, Grandma?" he asked.

"My Granddaughter will be here any minute," she said.
"Everyday with the picnics!
You never tasted such awful potato salad!
I need a rest, badly."
That gave the Wolf a very smart idea.

He gave grandma his train ticket and off to Florida she gratefully went! Meanwhile, the wolf stayed behind to greet Little Red Riding Hood; his very first friend.

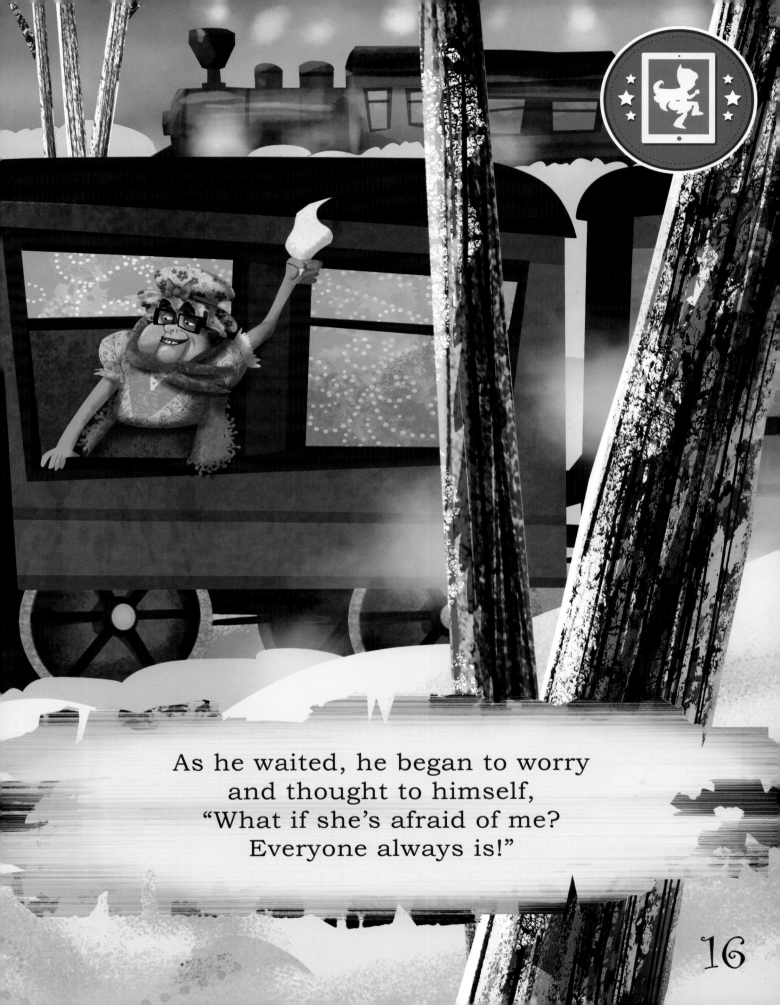

As he waited, he began to worry
and thought to himself,
"What if she's afraid of me?
Everyone always is!"

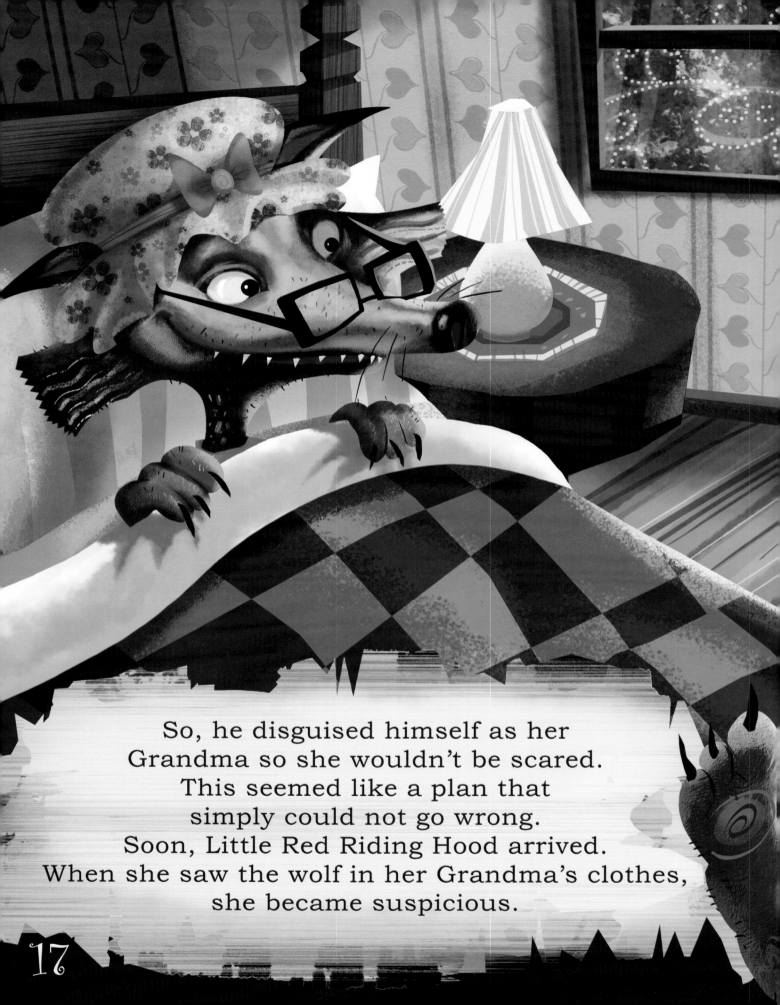

So, he disguised himself as her
Grandma so she wouldn't be scared.
This seemed like a plan that
simply could not go wrong.
Soon, Little Red Riding Hood arrived.
When she saw the wolf in her Grandma's clothes,
she became suspicious.

"Grandma, what big ears you have!"
she said, because when your
grandmother suddenly looks like a wolf,
you always notice the ears first.
"All the better to *hear* you with, my dear!" replied
the Wolf, pleased with his response.

18

"Grandma, what big eyes you have!"
said Little Red Riding Hood.
"All the better to see you with, my dear!" said
the Wolf, thinking that this was going pretty good.
"Grandma, what big teeth you have!" said
Little Red Riding Hood. "All the better to... to..."

Suddenly, the wolf couldn't think of anything to say, because his big teeth were meant for eating her. He was pretty sure saying that would make it harder for them to be friends.

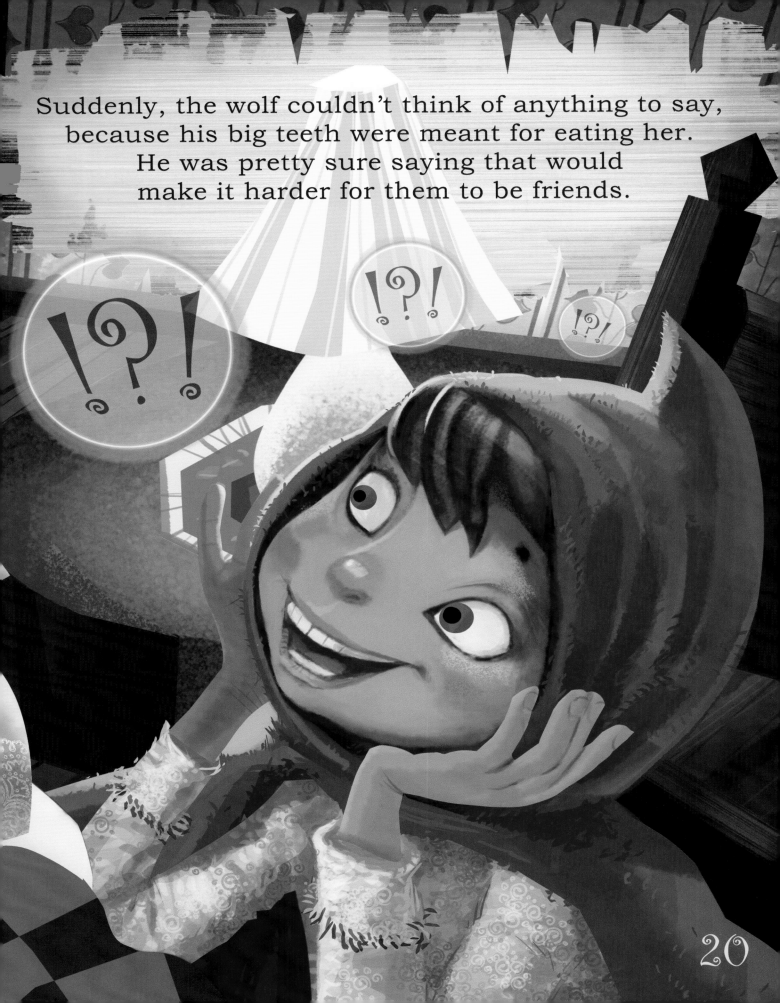

"I'm sorry, Little Red Riding Hood,"
the Wolf finally said.
"I'm not your Grandma. I'm Big Bad Wolf. Here,
I'll hold the door for you so you can run away.
I suggest screaming in the key of G.
That's the most popular."

21

Big Bad was surprised when
Little Red Riding Hood didn't run away,
because she was a very nice girl,
and she could see that he was sad.

22

"You don't look so very big,"
said Little Red Riding Hood,
"and you don't look so very bad either."
Then much to his surprise, she smiled.

"But where is my Grandma? She does love these picnics so. Don't tell her I said so, but I really don't like potato salad on these cold winter days." The Wolf smiled in reply. "Have you ever tried coconut?"

And they all lived happily ever after.

26

The End